LIFE IN THE AMERICAN COLONIES:
Daily Lifestyles of the Early Settlers

Edited by Jeanne Munn Bracken

1770 Colonial woman with rifle

Discovery Enterprises, Ltd.
Carlisle, Massachusetts

© Discovery Enterprises, Ltd., Carlisle, MA 1995
ISBN 1-878668-37-4 paperback edition

Library of Congress Catalog Card Number 95-68768

10 9 8 7 6 5 4 3

Printed in the United States of America

Cataloging in Publication Data

Life in the American Colonies:
Daily Lifestyles of the Early Settlers
edited by Jeanne Munn Bracken

United States — Social Life and Customs — To 1775

United States — History — Colonial period, c. 1600-1775

United States — Civilization — To 1783

Dewey Decimal No. 973.2

LC No. E 188

Photo/Illustration Credits

Cover Photo: This anonymous drawing depicts tradesmen
working at wood- cutting, tailoring, rolling, sewing, and grinding.
In the harbor are the watchful ships of the British.

Illustrations (pp. 8, 22, 28, 50), cropped from the originals found in
Colonial Living, The World Publishing Company, Cleveland, 1957.
Copyright Edwin Tunis.

Acknowledgments

The editor appreciates her library colleagues in Lincoln, Acton, and
Littleton, Massachusetts, and those with the Minuteman Library Network.
They enhance both of my lives—writer and librarian.

Table of Contents

Dedication

Often the writer-editor relationship is adversarial. I have been fortunate over the years in being able to work with excellent editors, but I have never dedicated a book to one.

The time has come. For her kindness and support, and for her belief in me, this book is dedicated to JoAnne B. Weisman of Discovery Enterprises, Ltd.

Foreword

"The migration to New England was a migration of communities already organized in England; the parish, crossing the ocean, became the township. ...Now the Dutch migration to New Netherland was not a migration of churches but of individuals. It brought with it no pre-existing organization. The resulting community was for a long time a fortuitous aggregation of traders ... and without that abiding interest in creating and sustaining homes which an agricultural community feels. This shifting mercantile community was governed by a commercial company whose prime interest in it was to make large dividends for its stockholders." — Fiske

"They were Puritans, Quakers, and Anglicans; they were English, French, Germans, and Scots; and they were dwelling in seaports and inland towns, on small farms and large plantations, in the tidewater, in the up-country, along the frontier, under temperate or semitropical skies."

As Charles M. Andrews writes, the American colonists were the first melting pot. In thinking about them, it is impossible to describe a "typical" colonist any more than we can describe a "typical American" today. Are we talking about a man or a woman? Perhaps about a child? Living in a town or on an isolated farm, or perhaps on a plantation? On the coast or pushing into the frontier? North or South? From Holland or England? Protestant, Catholic, or Jew? Free or slave? Poor or wealthy, or just plain middle-class? Is the year 1625 or 1770?

These are just a few of the considerations that define a time, a place and a people. It would be impossible to tell you everything about all the different colonists in a book this size, so let them speak as much as possible in their own words. These "primary sources" are writings from the pens of those who were there; they are fascinating but sometimes difficult to understand, with their strange spelling and language. Ann Hulton's description of the tar and feathering is a "primary source." We can also learn much from "secondary sources," experts who have studied the primary sources and then written about them. The excellent Alice Morse Earle books are secondary sources—and well worth reading.

So let us take a look at the colonists. Let this be a scrapbook with snapshots—momentary glimpses of our forefathers and foremothers as they created a new home in the New World.

The Colonial Homestead

*What did early settlements look like? New Amsterdam
(afterward New York) in 1648:*

"...Many ships from Holland brought loads of brick and tiles
as ballast, and the houses began to assume the typical Dutch
aspect. They were still built chiefly of wood, but with a gable
end of brick facing the street. ...The life of the family, as in
all primitive communities, was centered in the kitchen. Here
in winter roared the great fires up the wide-throated chimneys.
Here children and negro servants gathered in groups and told
stories of the old home and the new. Here the women knit
their stockings and here the burghers smoked when the day's
work was done." — Goodwin

"The making of the fire and its preservation from day to day
were of (great)...importance. The covering of the brands at night
was one of the domestic duties, whose non-fulfillment in those
matchless days often rendered necessary a journey with fire shovel
to the house of the nearest neighbor to obtain glowing coals to
start again the kitchen fire...

"The brick oven was not used so frequently, usually but once
a week...On one side of the kitchen fireplace, but really a part
of the chimney whole, was an oven which opened at one side
into the chimney... To heat this oven a great fire of dry wood
was kindled within it, and kept burning fiercely for some hours.
Then the coal and ashes were removed, the chimney draught and
damper were closed, and the food to be cooked was placed in the
heated oven. Great pans of brown bread, pots of pork and beans,
an Indian pudding a dozen pies, all went into the fierly furnace
together." — *Colonial Dames*

"One of the most important articles for setting the table was the trencher. These were made of wood, and often were only a block of wood, about ten or twelve inches square and three or four deep, hollowed down into a sort of bowl in the middle. In this the food was placed,—porridge, meat, vegetables, etc.

Trencher

Each person did not have even one of these simple dishes; usually two children, or a man and his wife, ate out of one trencher. ...I have seen a curious old table top, or table-board, which permitted diners seated at it to dispense with trenchers or plates. It was of heavy oak about six inches thick, and at intervals of about eighteen inches around its edge were scooped out deep, bowl-shaped holes about ten inches in diameter, in which each individual's share of the dinner was placed. After each meal the top was lifted off the trestles, thoroughly washed and dried, and was ready for the next meal... There was no attempt made to give separate drinking-cups of any kind to each individual at the table. Blissfully ignorant of the existence or presence of microbes, germs, and bacteria, our sturdy and unsqueamish forbears drank contentedly in succession from a single vessel, which was passed from hand to hand, and lip to lip, around the board. ...The bedrooms were seldom warmed and had it not been for the deep feather beds and heavy bed-curtains, would have been unendurable. In Dutch and some German houses, with alcove bedsteads, and sleeping on one feather bed, with another for cover, the Dutch settlers could be far warmer than any English settlers, even in four-post bedsteads curtained with woollen. Water froze immediately if left standing in bedrooms." — *Home Life*

"The deep dark cellar, with its coolish and even temperature, was for much more than half the year a storage-place for provisions... A large part of the autumn work was the preparation of the stores that were to be put away in the spacious cellar. The packing of butter in firkins and pickled pork in barrels, the smoking of hams and bacon, the corning of beef rounds and briskets, the chopping of sausage-meat and head-cheese, the trying of lard, the careful and dainty salting of mackerel and other fish,—made it a busy time for all the household. In the cellar might be found all these good things, with kegs of soused pigs' feet, stone jars of pickles, barrels of red and green apples, bins heaped high with potatoes, parsnips, and turnips; along with barrels of vinegar, cider, and ale, and...brown jugs of rum. In the houses of the wealthier sort there was also plenty of wine." — Fiske

North and South Colonies

"The towns of New England were compact little communities, favorably situated by sea or river, and their inhabitants were given over in the main to the pursuit of agriculture... Life in the towns was one of incessant activity. The New Englander's house, with its barns, outbuildings, kitchen garden, and back lot, fronted the village street, while near at hand were the meetinghouse and schoolhouse, pillories, stocks... Beyond this clustered group of houses stretched the outlying arable land, meadows, pastures, and woodlands, the scene of the villager's industry and the source of his livelihood. Thence came wheat and corn for his gristmill, hay and oats for his horses and cattle, timber for his sawmill, and wood for the huge fireplace which warmed his home. The lots of an individual owner would be scattered in several divisions, some near at hand, to be reached easily on foot, others two or more miles distant... The average New England country household was a sort of self-sustaining unit which depended little on the world beyond its own gates.

"...The Southerner was not used to small holdings and closely settled towns; his eye was accustomed to range over wide stretches of land filled with large estates and plantations. The clearings to which he was accustomed, though often little more than a third of the whole area, consisted of great fields of tobacco, grain, rice, and indigo (a dye plant), and presented an appearance essentially unlike that of the small and scattered lots and farms of the New England towns. He was unacquainted with the self-centered activity of those busy northern communities...

"In both (Maryland and Virginia) there were hundreds of small farmers possessing single grants of land upon which they had erected modest houses. Many of these farmers rented lands of the planter under limited leases and paid their rents in money, or probably more often in produce, labor and money...

"Most of the plantations of South Carolina and Georgia were smaller than those in Maryland and Virginia. A single tract rarely exceeded 2000 acres, and an entire property did not often include more than 5000 acres. These estates seem to have been on the whole more compact and less scattered than elsewhere. They lay contiguous to each other in many instances and formed large continuous areas of rice land, pine land, meadow, pasture, and swamp. Upon such plantations the colonists built substantial houses of brick and cypress, generally less elaborate than those in Virginia... There were also tanyards, distilleries, and soap-houses, as well as all facilities for raising rice, corn, and later indigo. At first the chief staple on these plantations was rice; but the introduction of indigo in 1745, with its requirement of vats, pumps, and reservoirs, and its plague of refuse and flies, though of great significance in restoring the prosperity of the province, gave rise to new and in some respects less agreeable conditions..." — Andrews

Families and Home Life

We have long been taught that these early settlers were religious dissenters, strict church-goers, Pilgrims. The word "Puritan" conjures an image of a stern, overly disciplined patriarch. Certainly some of the colonists were like that. But not all. There was also a good deal of difference among the different colonies and of course the "typical" colonist changed over time.

"Colonial marriages took place at even so early an age as fourteen; and the number of men and women who were married two, three, and four times was large. Instances of a thrice widower marrying a twice or thrice widow are not uncommon... Large families, even of twenty-six children (born to) a single mother, are recorded, but infant mortality was very great. ... (M)any mothers died early, and often in childbirth. ...Second marriages were the rule.

Families therefore very often consisted of stepchildren, stepparents, and multiple generations living under one roof—not unlike the situation in many homes today.

"...Divorces were rare... In the case of unhappy marriages, separation by mutual agreement was occasionally resorted to. Sometimes the lady ran away; and, indeed, advertisements for runaway wives seem almost as common in Southern newspapers as those for runaway servants." — Andrews

This ballad dates from about 1630, taking an honest look at life in the Plymouth colony.

Forefathers' Song

The place where we live is a wilderness wood,
Where grass is much wanting that's fruitful and good;
Our mountains and hills and our valleys below,
Being commonly covered with ice and with snow;
And when the north-west wind with violence blows,
Then every man pulls his cap over his nose;
But if any's so hardy and will it withstand,
He forfeits a finger, a foot or a hand.
But when the Spring opens we then take the hoe,
And make the ground ready to plant and to sow;
Our corn being planted and seed being sown,
The worms destroy much before it is grown;
And when it is growing, some spoil there is made
By birds and by squirrels that pluck up the blade;
And when it is come to full corn in the ear,
It is often destroyed by raccoon and by deer...
If fresh meat be wanting to fill up our dish,
We have carrots and turnips as much as we wish;
And if there's a mind for a delicate dish
We repair to the clam-banks, and there we catch fish.
...We have pumpkins at morning and pumpkins at noon,
If it were not for pumpkins we should be undone!
...We can make liquor to sweeten our lips,
Of pumpkins and parsnips and walnut-tree chips.
But you whom the Lord intends hither to bring,
Forsake not the honey for fear of the sting,
But bring both a quiet and contented mind,
And all needful blessings you surely will find.
— *Annals of America*, vol. 1

"The description of the first settlers (mid-1600s) at Wiltwyck on the western shore of the (Hudson) river may be applied to all the pioneer Dutch colonists. 'Most of them could neither read nor write. They were a wild, uncouth, rough, and most of the time a drunken crowd. They lived in small log huts, thatched with straw. They wore rough clothes, and in the winter were dressed in skins. They subsisted on a little corn, game, and fish. They were afraid of neither man, God, nor the Devil.'

"The wife of a typical settler was rough, coarse, ignorant, uncultivated. She helped her husband to build their log hut, to plant his grain, and to gather his crops. If Indians appeared in her husband's absense, she grasped the rifle, gathered her children about her, and with a dauntless courage defended them even unto death." — Goodwin

"In the South...(slaves) in the house wore blue jacket and breeches and those in the field generally white. ...When a servant or negro ran away, he put on everything that he had or could steal, and such a fugitive must have been a grotesque sight. One runaway servant is described as wearing a gray rabbit-skin hat with a clasp to it, a periwig of bright brown hair, a close serge coat, breeches of brownish color, worsted stockings, and wooden heeled shoes..." — Andrews

Colonial Diet

The colonial diet was both more varied and less so than we might think. Since preservation techniques were limited, much food had to be consumed when it was fresh. In the winter, meals could be very monotonous.

"Nearly all the meats, vegetables and fruits familiar to house-keepers of today (1900) were known to the colonial dames. In the better houses, beef, mutton, lamb, pork, ham, bacon, and smoked and dried fish were eaten as well as sausages, cheese, and butter, which were usually homemade... As for vegetables,

14

the New Englander was familiar with cabbages, radishes, lettuce, turnips, green corn, carrots, parsnips, spinach, onions, beets, parsley, savory, mustard, peppergrass, celery, cauliflower, squashes, pumpkins, beans, peas, and asparagus; but only the more prosperous householders pretended to cultivate even a majority of these in their gardens. In the rural districts, only cabbages, beans, pumpkins, and other vegetables of the coarser varieties were grown... In the South sweet potatoes early became popular, and watermelons and muskmelons were raised in large quantities...

"Fruit was abundant everywhere. Apples, pears, peaches, apricots, damsons, plums, quinces, cherries, and crab apples were all raised in the orchards, North and South, while oranges, probably small and very sour, were grown in South Carolina and...East Florida... Of the smaller fruits, strawberries, blackberries, and gooseberries were cultivated and highly prized; wild strawberries and huckleberries were as well known as they are now; and grapes were found in enormous quantities in a wild state, though efforts to grow vineyards for the purpose of making wine were never very successful." — Andrews

"Potatoes were known to New Englanders but were rare... It was believed by many persons that if a man ate (potatoes) every day, he could not live seven years... A fashionable way of cooking them was with butter, sugar, and grape-juice; this was mixed with dates, lemons, and mace; seasoned with cinnamon, nutmeg, and pepper; then covered with a frosting of sugar—and you had to hunt well to find the potato among all these other things. ... Preserving (food) was a very different art from canning fruit today. Vast jars were filled with preserves so rich that there was no need of keeping air from them; they could be opened, that is, the paper cover taken off, and used as desired; there was no fear of fermentation, souring, or moulding... They candied fruits and nuts, made many marmalades...and a vast number of fruit wines

and cordials. They...potted many kinds of fish and game, and they salted and soused (pickled). There were many families that found all their supply of sweetening in maple sugar and honey; but housewives of dignity and elegance desired to have some supply of sugar, certainly to offer visitors for their dish of tea. This sugar was always loaf sugar...for it was purchased ever in great loaves or cones which averaged in weight about nine to ten pounds apiece. One cone would last thrifty folk for a year."
— *Home Life*

Recipes were sometimes written in rhyme, as the following shows. Sack was a cheap Spanish wine used in the colonies for a sack-posset traditionally drunk by the bride and groom. This recipe dates to the mid-1700s. (Note that it calls for eggs from a cock, or rooster; now that's poetic license!)

Sack-Posset

From famed Barbadoes on the Western Main
Fetch sugar half a pound; fetch sack from Spain
A pint; and from the Eastern Indian Coast
Nutmeg, the glory of our Northern toast.
O'er flaming coals together let them heat
Till the all-conquering sack dissolves the sweet.
O'er such another fire set eggs, twice ten,
New born from crowing cock and speckled hen;
Stir them with steady hand, and conscience pricking
To see the untimely fate of twenty chicken.
From shining shelf take down your brazen skillet,
A quart of milk from gentle cow will fill it.
When boiled and cooked, put milk and sack to egg,
Unite them firmly like the triple League,
Then covered close, together let them dwell
Till Miss twice sings: You must not kiss and tell.
Each lad and lass snatch up their murdering spoon,
And fall on fiercely like a starved dragoon.
— *Stage Coach*

16

Colonial Names

In this era of Jasons and Jennifers, the names of many of the colonists seem very odd.

"Dame Dineley, widow of a doctor or barber-surgeon who had died in the snow while striving to visit a distant patient, named her poor babe Fathergone... Comfort, Deliverance, Temperance, Peace, Hope, Patience, Charity, Faith, Love, Submit, Endurance, Silence, Joy, Rejoice, Hoped for, and similar names indicative of a trait of character, a virtue, or an aspiration of goodness, were common. The children of Roger Clap were named Experience, Waitstill, Preserved, Hopestill, Wait, Thanks, Desire, Unite and Supply. Madam Austin...had sixteen children. Their names were Parvis, Picus, Piersus, Prisemus, Polybius, Lois, Lettice, Avis, Anstice, Eunice, Mary, John, Elizabeth, Ruth, Freelove... Richard Gridley's offspring were Return, Believe, and Tremble."
— *Child Life*

Children

Some of the colonial ideas about child-rearing seem pretty odd today. Philosopher John Locke's Thoughts on Education, *an English book published in 1690, was a popular early version of Dr. Spock. The advice, however, was not.*

"One of Locke's instructions much thought on in the years his book was so widely read was the advice to wash the child's feet daily in cold water. Josiah Quincy was the suffering subject of some of this instruction; when only three years old he was taken from his warm bed in winter as well as summer (and this in Eastern Massachusetts), carried downstairs to a cellar kitchen and dipped three times in a tub of cold water fresh from the pump. ...

This was a rather radical idea, since our forefathers and foremothers were not known for their regular bathing habits. Water of course had to be carried from a spring or pump and heated over an open fire. This was a lot of work, so the colonists were satisfied with washing face and hands and occasionally other body parts with cold water. Even that must have been an ordeal in their unheated homes, when water in basins even set close to the fire sometimes froze. Quincy, incidently, apparently suffered no ill effects, since he later served as Mayor of Boston and President of Harvard College.

Locke also had firm ideas about a child's diet.

"'(Meat) should be (avoided) ...at least till (the boy) is two or three years old.' If the boy called for victuals between meals, he should have dry bread. His only extra drink should be small-beer, which should be warm; and seldom should he taste wine or strong drink. Locke would not have children eat melons, peaches, plums or grapes...The bed should be hard, of quilts rather than feathers."
— *Child Life*

"Children in many households were not allowed to sit...while eating. Many times they had to stand by the side of the table during the entire meal... In some families children stood behind their parents and other grown persons, and food was handed back to them from the table... This seems closely akin to throwing food to an animal... The chief thought on the behavior of children at the table...is that they were to eat in silence, as fast as possible (regardless of indigestion), and leave the table as speedily as might be. ...They were ordered never to seat themselves at the table until after the blessing had been asked, and their parents told them to be seated. They were never to ask for anything on the table; never to speak unless spoken to; always to break the bread, not to bite into a whole slice; never to take salt except with a clean knife; not to throw bones under the table.

"The dress of little girls in families of wealth was certainly almost as formal and elegant as the dress of their mammas... They wore vast hoop-petticoats, heavy stays, and high-heeled shoes... Little Dolly Payne, who afterwards became the wife of President Madison, went to school wearing 'a white linen mask to keep every ray of sunshine from the complexion, a sunbonnet sewed on her head every morning by her careful mother, and long gloves covering the hands and arms.' " — *Home Life*

Cavalier   Puritan   Hollander   Quaker

Costumes of the early settlers

Education

An early consideration for some of the colonists was education. The sons of wealthier families were sent back to Europe for schooling. Towns established schools, but those children living too far away were tutored instead. The first college in the British colonies was established at Cambridge, Massachusetts, in 1636, with funds from the General Court—half of the colony's annual income! Thus Harvard College became the first institution of higher education anywhere in the world to be created by a representative body of the public using public funds.

"The first schoolmaster sent to New Netherland arrived in 1633...Adam Roelantsen was twenty-seven years old when he was sent over seas as instructor of youth in the colony, and he was as precious a scoundrel as ever was set to teach the young. He eked out his slender income in the early days by taking in washing or by establishing a bleachery, which must be noted as one of the most creditable items in his scandalous career. He was constantly before the local courts of New Amsterday, sometimes as plaintiff, sometimes as defendant, and finally he appeared as a malefactor charged with so grave an offense that the court declared...'we condemn said Roelantsen to be flogged and banished forever out of this country.' Apparently, on the plea of having four motherless children, he escaped the infliction of punishment and continued alternately to amuse and to outrage the respectable burghers of New Amsterdam.

The Dutch schoolmasters also had to take the children to church.

"...the official schoolmaster was pledged 'to promote religious worship, to read a portion of the word of God to the people, to endeavor, as much as possible to bring them up in the ways of the Lord, to console them in their sickness, and to conduct himself with all diligence and fidelity in his calling, so as to give others a good example as becometh a devout, pious and worth consoler of the sick, church-clerk,...and School master.' " — Goodwin

It is no wonder that Roelantsen couldn't live up to these standards.

Even the youngest children, both boys and girls, went sometimes to dame schools. These were a sort of nursery school run by women in their homes, who taught their pupils to read.

"The pay of teachers who taught the dame-schools was meagre in the extreme. The town of Woburn, Massachusetts, reached the lowest ebb of salary. In 1641 a highly respected widow, one Mrs. Walker, kept a school in a room of her own house. The town agreed to pay her ten shillings for the first year; but after deducting seven shillings for taxes, and various small amounts for produce, etc., she received finally from the town *one shilling and three pence* for her pedagogical work.

"In New England, where the population was concentrated in and around villages, it was possible for the town to maintain schools, either public or private, as the case might be... In Virginia and the colonies south of that region this was very difficult, for the simple reason that the population was too widely scattered. In very few places were there enough children within the radius of possible school attendance to form even a small school. The result of this condition was that the great planters who wished to educate their children were compelled to employ tutors and governesses of their own." — Eggleston

21

A colonial schoolroom

"While the education of the sons of the planters in all the colonies was bravely provided and supported, the daughters fared but poorly. The education of a girl in book learning was deemed of vastly less importance than her instruction in household duties.

"...it is pathetic to read of a learning-hungry little maid in Hatfield, Massachusetts, who would slip away from her spinning and knitting and sit on the schoolhouse steps to listen with eager envy to the boys as they recited within.

Colonial learning methods would seem foreign to today's students. Rather than books, the pupils learned the alphabet and spelling from a hornbook.

"A thin piece of wood, usually about four or five inches long and two inches wide, had placed upon it a sheet of paper a trifle smaller, printed at the top with the alphabet in large and small letters; below were simple syllables such as ab, eb, ib, ob, etc.; then came the Lord's Prayer. This printed page was covered with a thin sheet of yellowish horn, which was not as transparent as glass, yet permitted the leters to be read through it... It was, therefore, a book of a single page..." — *Child Life*

From John Newbery's A Little Pretty Pocket-Book, *an example of one of the rhymed fables with its moral lesson:*

Fable III
The Shepherd's Boy

A Wanton young *Shepherd,*
    Tho' no Danger near,
Cries out to his Neighbours,
    The *Wolf,* Sirs, is here.
They come, and are laugh'd at;
    Soon he roars out again,
Now the *Wolf's* here indeed,
    But his cries are in vain

To *Master* Tommy, or *Miss* Polly.

This Boy's Fate, my Dear, is a remarkable instance of the Folly and Wickedness of telling Lies; if he had not deceived the People before, they would have believed him, and ran to his Assistance, by which Means both he and his Sheep might have been saved, which are now torn to Pieces; I hope you'll remember this, my Dear, and resolve in yourself never to tell a Lie; for if you do, I shall be very angry. I am, Your hearty Friend, Jack the Giant-Killer.

As is obvious from the inclusion of the Lord's Prayer on the hornbooks, there was no question of separating the church from the public schools. Teachers were expected to instruct in morals and the Bible as well as reading and simple arithmetic. Such books as existed were heavily religious stories like John Bunyan's Pilgrim's Progress. *Even the simple primers that replaced the hornbooks in schoolrooms were based on Biblical writings and daily prayers.*

"The fashion of the day was to set everything in rhyme as an aid to memory; and even so unpoetical a subject as English Grammar did not escape the rhyming writer. In the *Grammer of the English Tongue*, a large and formidable book in fine type, all the rules and lists of exceptions and definitions were in verse. A single specimen, the definition of a letter, will show the best style of composition, which, when it struggled with moods and tenses, was absolutely meaningless.

'A Letter is an uncompounded Sound
Of which there no Division can be Found,
Those Sounds to Certain Characters we fix,
Which in the English Tongue are Twenty-Six.'

Spelling was "wildly varied" in those days and not standardized until Noah Webster issued his American Spelling Book *in 1783. With all the students chanting their lessons in unison, the din could be deafening—and not just within the school.*

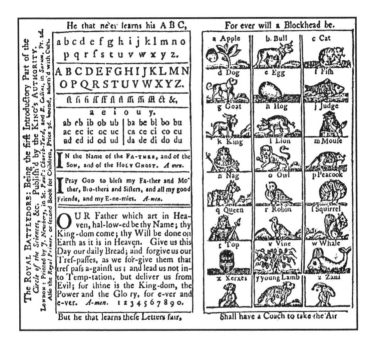

"The roar of the many voices of the large school, all pitched in different keys, could be heard on summer days for a long distance. In many country schools the scholars not only spelled aloud but studied all their lessons aloud...; and the teacher was quick to detect any lowering of the volume of sound and would reprove any child who was studying silently. Sometimes the combined roar of voices became offensive to the neighbors of the school, and restraining votes were passed at town-meetings.

What constituted good manners was quite a bit different two centuries ago. The child's expected behavior at school was minutely described:

"...to take off his hat at entering, and bow to the teacher; to rise up and bow at the entrance of any stranger; to 'bawl not in speaking'; to 'walk not cheek by jole' (side by side) but fall respectfully behind...

By the eve of the American Revolution, Harvard had company in providing higher education to the sons of the colonists.

"Harvard was established in 1636; William and Mary in Virginia in 1693; Yale in Connecticut in 1700; Princeton (in New Jersey) in 1746; King's College (Columbia) in New York City—1754; the College of Philadelphia (now the University of Pennsylvania) in 1755; Brown University at Providence, Rhode Island, in 1764; Dartmouth in New Hampshire in 1769; Rutgers in New Jersey in 1770." — Eggleston

Church

*Since a great many of the earliest colonists came to America
seeking religious freedom, it is not surprising that church would
play such a major role in their lives. There was no attempt at all
to separate church from state. The first public building erected in
each colony was a meeting-house, used for worship and for government. Attendance at services was often required and church
funds were raised by taxes.*

"There were many public offices in colonial times which
we do not have to-day, for we do not need them. One of these is
that of tithing-man; he was a town officer, and had several neigh-
boring families under his charge... He enforced the learning of
the church catechism in these ten homes, visited the houses,
and heard the children recite their catechism. These ten families
he watched specially on Sundays to see whether they attended
church... In some Massachusetts towns he watched on week
days to keep 'boys and all persons from swimming in the water.'
Ten families with many boys must have kept him busy on hot
August days. He inspected taverns, reported disorderly persons,
and forbade the sale of intoxicating liquor to them. He adminis-
tered the 'oath of fidelity' to new citizens, and warned undesirable visitors and wanderers to leave the town. He could arrest
persons who ran or rode at too fast a pace when going to meeting
on Sunday, or who took unnecessary rides on Sunday, or other-
wise broke the Sunday laws.

"Within the meeting-house he kept order by...correcting unruly and noisy boys, and waking those who slept. He sometimes
walked up and down the church aisles, carrying a stick which had
a knob on one end, and a dangling foxtail on the other, tapping
the boys on the head with the knob end of the stick, and tickling
the face of sleeping church attendants with the foxtail.

A New England Meetinghouse

Sundays, particularly in the earliest days, were a very serious day with strict rules of what could be done (Bible reading, church attendance) and what couldn't be done (almost everything else). The story is told of an old Deacon Davis of Westborough, Massachusetts:

"A grandson walked to church with him one Sabbath morning and a gray squirrel ran across the road. The child, delighted, pointed out the beautiful little creature to his grandfather. A sharp twist of the ear was the old Puritan's (response), and the (sharp) words that 'squirrels were not to be spoken of on the Lord's Day.' " — *Child Life*

"The first meeting-houses were often decorated in a very singular and grotesque manner. Rewards were paid by all the early towns for killing wolves; and any person who killed a wolf brought the head to the meeting-house and nailed it to the outer walls; the fierce grinning heads and splashes of blood made a grim and horrible decoration." — *Home Life*

"The meetinghouse, usually built of wood...was situated in the center of town. It was at first a plain, unadorned, rectangular structure, sometimes painted and sometimes not, without tower or steeple...

"...The interior was usually bare and unattractive; the pulpit stood on one side high above the pews...The body of the house was filled with high square pews... Assignment of pews followed social rank; front seats were reserved for the deacons; convenient (seats) were set apart for the deaf; the side seats were for those of lesser (status) and the gallery for the children. In these meeting-houses there were neither fires nor lights...In the winter season the chill of the building must have imperiled the lives of those unlucky infants whose fate it was to be baptized with icy waters." — Andrews

"These narrow, shelf-like seats (around the sides of the pews) were usually hung on hinges and could be turned up against the pew-walls during the long psalm-tunes and prayers; so the members of the congregation could lean against the pew-walls for support as they stood. When the seats were let down, they fell with a heavy slam that could be heard half a mile away in the summer time when the windows of the meeting-house were open... The churches were all unheated...Dogs...were permitted to enter the meeting-house and lie on their masters' feet. Dog-whippers or dog-pelters were appointed to control and expel them when they became unruly or unbearable. Women and children usually carried foot-stoves, which were little pierced metal boxes that stood on wooden legs and held hot coals." — *Home Life*

"The minister was truly the leader of his people. He comforted and reproved them, guided their spiritual footsteps, advised them in matters domestic and civil... He was the chief citizen of the town, reverenced by the old and regarded with something akin to awe by the young.

"...(Sermons)...were blunt and often terrifying; and in language which was plain, ernest and uncompromising they (preached) against such human weaknesses as swearing, drunkenness, fornication, and sleeping in church. Sermons almost always lasted at least an hour, and "sermons of two hours were not unknown." — Andrews

Work

Everyone worked in the colonies as soon as they were considered old enough—and that was at a very young age.

"Colonial children did not spend much time in play... It was ordered by the magistrates that children tending sheep or cattle in the field should be 'set to some other employment (as well), such as spinning upon the rock, knitting, weaving tape, etc.'

"There was plenty of work on a farm even for little children; they sowed various seeds in early spring; they weeded flax fields, walking barefoot among the tender plants; they hetchelled flax and combed wool.

"Knitting was taught to little girls as soon as they could hold the needles. Girls four years of age could knit stockings and mittens..." — *Child Life*

Boys did learn to knit but their other chores were different. They sawed and chopped wood, threshed grain, helped make cider and soap; made birch splinter brooms (often to earn a little pocket money), gathered nuts, and with their jack-knives whittled all manner of things for outdoor and hearthside use.

We tend to think of women as homebodies or house servants in the colonial era, but that was not true.

"Women kept (taverns) from early days. Widows abounded, for the life of the male colonists was hard, exposure was great, and many died in middle age. War also had many victims. Tavern-keeping was the resort of widows of small means then, just as the 'taking of boarders' (was later). Women were skilled in business affairs and competent; many licenses were granted to them to keep victualling-houses, to draw wine, and make and sell beer." — *Stage-Coach*

"In 1670 a Boston woman was licensed to sell coffee and chocolate, and soon coffee houses were established there. Some did not know how to cook coffee...but boiled the whole coffee-beans in water, ate them, and drank the liquid; and naturally this was not very good either to eat or drink." — *Home Life*

"The taverns of Boston were the original business exchanges; they combined the Counting House, the Exchange-office, the Reading-room, and the bank..." — *Stage-Coach*

From the earliest days, town dwellers fell asleep to the sounds of the night watchman. This colonist was a cross between fire warden, policeman and clock tower, calling out the time and the weather.

"When the curfew (in New Amsterdam) rang (eight o'clock) from the belfry, lights were put out and all was made fast for the night, while the children's minds were set at rest by the tramp of the klopperman, who shook his rattle at each door as he passed from house to house through the dark hours, assuring the burghers that all was well and that no marauders were about." — Goodwin

Jack of All Trades

Colonists had to master many skills in order to survive, but one gentleman must have been something of a curiosity.

"Joshua Hempstead of New London (Connecticut)...was not only a farmer but at one time or another, from 1711 to 1753, a housebuilder, carpenter, and cabinetmaker, shipwright, cobbler, maker of coffins, and engraver of tombstones, a town official holding the offices of selectman, treasurer, assessor, and surveyor of highways; a colony official, serving as deputy sheriff and coroner, many times deputy to the General Court, justice of the peace, and so performing frequent marriages, and judge of probate. He was also clerk of the ecclesistical society... and surveyor of lands. He did a great deal of legal business, drawing deeds, leases, wills, and other similar documents, and was general handy man for his community."

Whew!

Labor Force

Many of the colonists were unable to afford their passage to America. Instead, they signed on with ship captains, who brought them to North America. Once here, their labor was sold for a certain number of years, depending on their age and how many family members came along—and how many of that family were able to work. These were "indentured" servants. Not all came willingly; some were kidnapped in seaports and forced to come to America.

"Land and living were cheap in this tobacco land, but labor was needed for the crops...warm invitations were sent back to England for all and every kind of labor. Convicts were welcomed... Landlords were even granted lands in proportion to their number of servants; a hundred acres per capita was the allowance. It can readily be seen that an ambitious or unscrupulous planter would gather in some way as many heads as possible.

"The kidnapped servants did not fare badly. Many examples are known where they worked on until they had acquired ample means...Still...(c)heap ballads were sold in England warning English maidens against kidnapping.

"To prevent enticing or kidnapping, all servants were registered before sailing and sometimes, as at Bristol, where the mayor and aldermen interfered, the ship was searched before sailing, the passengers were ordered ashore, and all who wished were released." — Andrews

"A woman (arriving by ship) must (serve the indenture) for her husband if he arrives sick, and, in like manner, a man for his sick wife, and take the debt upon herself or himself, and thus serve five to six years, not alone for his or her own debt but also for that of the sick husband or wife. ...It often happens that whole families—husband, wife, and children—are separated by being sold to different purchasers, especially when they have not paid any part of their passage money.

"When both parents have died over halfway at sea, their children, especially when they are young and have nothing to pawn or to pay, must stand for their own and their parents' passage, and serve till they are twenty-one years old."
— *Annals of America*, vol. 2

"Children began the period of their service sometimes at the early age of ten. The abilities of these imported servants varied greatly; many were laborers, others were artisans and tradesmen, and a few were trained workmen possessed of exceptional skill. Among them were dyers, tailors, upholsterers, weavers, joiners, carpenters, cabinetmakers, barbers, shoemakers, peruke maers, ...blacksmiths, coachmen, gentlemen's servants, gardeners, bakers, house waiters, schoolteachers, and even doctors and surgeons." — Andrews

"The indentured servant...saw before him, at the close of his seven years term, a home in a teeming land; he would own fifty acres of that land with three barrels, an axe, a gun, and a hoe—truly, the world was his... (An indentured woman servant) had an equal start, a petticoat and waistcoat of strong wool...two blue aprons, two linen caps, a pair of new shoes, two pairs of new stockings and a smock, and three barrels of Indian corn."
— *Two Centuries*

Another form of hired labor was apprenticeship—signing on with a craftsman to learn his trade over a period of years.

"Sometimes an apprentice was scarcely to be distinguished from an indentured servant, as when a minor bound himself to serve until a debt was paid off. Apprenticeship proved a useful sort of service in the colonies, for, though it was at times much abused and both masters and apprentices complained that the contracts were not carried out, it trained good workmen and satisfied a real need.

"Though originally in quite a different position, the transported prisoner was in much the same condition as the servant and apprentice, for he too was a laborer bound to service without pay for a given number of years. ...Not less than 40,000 of these convicts were sent between the years 1717 and 1775 to the colonies, chiefly to Pennsylvania, Maryland, Virginia and the West Indies. Some were transported for seven years, some for fourteen, and some for life, and though the colonies protested and (some) passed laws against the practice, the need of labor was so great that convicts continued to be received and were sometimes even smuggled across the borders of the colony. Determined to get rid of an undesirable social element, England hoped in this way to lessen the number of executions at home and to turn to good account the skill and physical strength of able-bodied men and women. When a certain Englishman argued in favor of transporting felons for the purpose of reforming them, (Ben) Franklin is said to have retaliated by suggesting the reformation of American rattlesnakes by sending them to England.

"As convicts were often transported for very slight offenses, it is stated that, at times when conditions were very bad in the mother country, the starving poor, rather than continue to suffer, would commit trifling thefts for which transportation was the penalty. Thus though there were many who were confirmed criminals, those who had been merely petty offenders were distinctly advantageous to the colonies as artisans and laborers." — Andrews

As time passed and especially as the plantation system developed in the South, a larger labor force was needed to tend the rice, tobacco, indigo and later cotton crops. These workers were also kidnapped and brought to America against their will—as African slaves.

The slaves were not educated as a general rule; in fact, law often forbade teaching them to read and write. One exception was a boy of eleven, later called Gustavus Vasa who was captured in his native Benin and brought to Virginia. In later years he published his life story. Here is part of his account of his trip to the New World.

"I was soon put down under the decks, and there I received such a salutation in my nostrils as I had never experienced in my life; so that, with the loathsomeness of the stench, and crying together, I became so sick and low that I was not able to eat, nor had I the least desire to taste anything ... but soon, to my grief, two of the white men offered me eatables; and, on my refusing to eat, one of them held me fast by the hands, and laid me across, I think, the windlass, and tied my feet, while the other flogged me severely. ...

"...They gave me to understand we were to be carried to these white people's country to work for them. I then was a little revived, and thought, if it were no worse than working, my situation was not so desperate: but still I feared I should be put to death, the white people looked and acted, as I thought, in so savage a manner; for I had never seen among any people such instances of brutal cruelty; and this not only shewn towards us blacks but also to some of the whites themselves. One white man in particular I saw, when we were permitted to be on deck, flogged so unmercifully with a large rope...that he died in consequence of it; and they tossed him over the side as they would have done a brute. This made me fear these pepole the more; and I expected nothing less than to be treated in the same manner. — Katz

"The estates for the raising of rice or indigo were wholly in charge of overseers of such fibre as lash in hand could compel exhausting labour in malarious ditches from great gangs of 'Heathen Africans,' usually freshly imported, and still in wild resentment over their kidnapping and transportation. The cultivation of both rice and indigo was a deadly occupation; but a strapping negro could earn more than his price--then about forty pounds--within a year. It was actually more profitable to work him to death than to take care of him. Assuming, then, that human nature in South Carolina was neither better nor worse than in other parts of the civilised world, it is easy to see that (reductions) in their numbers, due to whatever cause, were easily repaired by fresh importations from Africa." — Smith

Female slaves in the tobacco field, under the watchful eye of the overseer. (Courtesy: Maryland Historical Society)

Recreation

The earliest colonists had no time for recreation; they were too busy trying to make homes for themselves in a difficult environment. Their leisure time, such as it was, was spent in church. Those who were caught "idling", even on Sunday, were often punished. Even as time passed, recreation for the colonists often had an element of work: the quilting bee, the barn raising, the apple paring party all involved "many hands" making "light work."

"A pioneer life means hard work for children as well as for their elders, and in the early years there was little time for play on the part of youthful New Netherlanders. As prosperity advanced and as negro servants were introduced, the privileges of childhood were extended and we find accounts of their sliding on their sleds down the hills of Fort Orange (Albany) and skating at New Amsterdam on the Collect Pond... The skates were of the type used in Holland, very long with curves at the front and rear, and, when metal could not be obtained, formed of ox-bone...

"If winter offered sports and pastimes, spring, summer, and autumn had each its own pleasures, fishing and clam digging, shooting and trapping, games with ball and slings, berry picking, and the gathering of peaches which fell so thickly that the very hogs refused them." — Goodwin

An eighteenth century boy plays with his kite.

When the youngsters could slip away, they played singing games like "Here we go round the mulberry bush," "ring around a rosy" and "London Bridge is falling down." What toys they had were hand-made.

"In the beautiful and cleanly needles of the pine the children had an unlimited supply for the manufacture of toys. Pretty necklaces could be made for personal adornment, resembling in miniature the fringed bark garments of the South Sea Islanders, and tiny brooms for dolls' houses. A thickly growing cluster of needles was called a 'lady.' When her petticoats were carefully trimmed, she could be placed upright on a sheet of paper, and by softly blowing upon it could be made to dance." — *Child Life*

Probably the first book for children that was intended for amusement as well as education was John Newbery's A Little Pretty Pocket-Book *(1744). Decorated with woodcuts, the book gave directions for popular games in rhyme as well as an ABC and a few fables (with morals, of course)—all written in rhyme. Shuttle-cock was similar to badminton.*

Shuttle-Cock

The Shuttle-Cock struck
    Does backward rebound;
But, if it be miss'd,
    It falls to the Ground.

Moral

Thus chequer'd in Life,
    As Fortune does flow;
Her Smiles lift us high,
    Her Frowns sink us low.

Swimming

When the Sun's Beams have warm'd the Air,
Our Youth to some cool Brook repair;
In whose refreshing Streams they play,
To the last Remnant of the Day.

Rule of Life.

Think ere you speak; for Words, once flown,
Once utter'd, are no more your own.

"On the occasion (of colonial fairs), horses, oxen, cows, sheep, hogs, and sundry sorts of goods were...for sale. The people indulged in such varieties of sport as a slow hirse race with a silver watch to the hindmost...a race with men in bags, and an obstacle race for boys...There were also such other amusing entertaiments as grinning contests by half a dozen men or women... and whistling contests...in which the participants were to whistle selected tunes as clearly as possible without laughing. The people enjoyed puppet shows...and fortune telling; and the...medicine hawker sold his wares from a stage and...always attracted a crowd. The fairs were also utilized in Virginia as an occasion for paying debts, trading horses, buying land...

"Prominent among more aristocratic colonial diversions were the balls and assemblies given in private and public houses, where dancing was the order of the evening. Dancing, though not strictly forbidden in New England, was not encouraged, particularly if it were promiscucous or mixed. ...

"Music, which was a popular colonial accomplishment, was taught as an important subject in a number of schools, and many a daughter was kept at her scales until she cried from sheer exhaustion. In the South the colonists were familiar with such musical instruments as the spinnet, harpsichord, pianoforte, viol, violin, violoncello, guitar, German flute, French horn, and jew's harp." — Andrews

Health and Sickness

"From infancy to old age death took ample toll—so great was colonial disregard for the laws of sanitation, so little the attention paid to drainage and disinfection...Medicinal herbs were dispensed by Indian doctors, and popular concoctions were taken in large doses by credulous people. ...(Q)uack remedies and proprietary medicines made by secret formula were very common.

"Of indoor bathing it is difficult to find any trace. There were bathing pools on some of the Southern plantations, and swimming holes abounded...but probably bathtubs were entirely unknown and "washing" was as far as the colonists' ablutions went.

"The toothbrush had not yet been invented, but tooth washes and tooth powders were in use as early as 1718. ...Salt and water was the commonest dentifrice (rubbed on with a cloth). That these ... were not very successful is evident from the prevalent toothache and decay which necessitated frequent pulling and an early resort to false teeth... The goldsmiths advertised false teeth for sale." — Andrews

"It must be borne in mind that in colonial times no city in all the land had any proper water supply. The people got their water from wells dug within the city itself. These wells were necessarily contaminated by drainage from the reeking streets and from other and still fouler sources, for there were no sewers to carry off drainage, no plumbing in houses, nothing indeed in the way of municipal sanitation, except the maintenance of the corporation hogs to eat what they might of the filth of the streets and still further to foul them. It is no wonder that the death rate in American cities in the colonial period appears to have been appalling, compensated for only by the tendency to large families..." — Eggleston

"The early settlers found much difficulty in enforcing public sanitation for...we find the burghers in 1658 bitterly reproached for throwing their rubbish, filth, dead animals, and the like into the streets 'to the great inconvenience of the community and dangers arising from it.' The burgomasters...ordained that all such refuse be brought to dumping-grounds near the City hall and the gallows or to other designated places..." — Goodwin

"Smallpox was always prevalent, so much so that a person whose face showed no pittings was deemed almost a curiosity. Vaccination was not discovered by Jenner in England until near the end of the eighteenth century, but during the colonial period it was the general practice to innoculate persons with smallpox itself, after careful preparation, in order that they might have the disease under favorable circumstances, and thus escape the risk of having it later in unfavorable conditions. It was the custom for a number of friends to organize themselves into a smallpox party, take quarters together in the house of an inoculator, and there go through the experience in each other's company.

"...The ventilation of sleeping rooms by night was regarded as dangerous... Benjamin Franklin on one occasion made a journey across country in company with John Adams. Stopping overnight at a rural inn the two were put to sleep in a single bed, after the tavern custom of that time. Franklin desired to open a window, but John Adams objected on the ground that it was dangerous to breath the 'damp night air.' Franklin as a scientist knew better, and assured his companion that the night air was in fact no damper than the air of the daytime, but Adams could not reconcile himself to the belief that it was safe to sleep in a room with an open window. So Franklin humored him until he went to sleep. Then (Ben) slipped out of bed, and without making any noise opened the window to its full extent. The next morning Adams declared that he had rarely slept so well or so comfortably, whereupon Franklin called his attention to the fact that he had slept in the midst of fresh air which had come through the surreptitiously opened window. Adams regarded the discovery as so important that he wrote a letter about it.

"The doctors of that time...knew nothing of the causes of disease. If a man had a fever they bled him until the fever abated. ...If a man had an intestinal trouble which the doctor of to-day would diagnosticate as appendicitis, they let him die, and called it cramp colic. ...In dealing with wounds their methods were crude and even cruel. They knew nothing of anesthetics and their knowledge even of the disinfection of wounds was crude... For example...if a man had a wound in his leg or his arm which required (amputation), the amputation was done by the surgeon without the administration of anything that might ease the pain and at the end of it the stump of the amputated limb was plunged into hot tar. This prevented destructive inflammation, but it involved an enormous amount of suffering on the part of the patient.

"Many of the doctors of that time were acquainted with less than a dozen drugs. They knew little of anatomy, nothing of chemistry, and almost nothing of hygiene." — Eggleston

Native American Relations

As with other aspects of colonial life, there was no "typical" relationship with the Native Americans. Jamestown in the winter of 1607 was stricken with starvation and disease; half of the colonists died, and more surely would have succumbed without the help of the Native Americans in their area. The struggling colony at Plymouth was also aided by friendly Native Americans.

"The freezing, starving company of Pilgrims, who might have been annihilated in a few minutes, were not approached (by natives) until spring. Then one day, to their amazement, a swarthy visitor greeted them in their mother-tongue with 'Welcome, Englishmen.' He was Samoset. Soon came Squanto, who said, in broken English, (that) he had been one of twenty natives taken to England by Captain Hunt in 1614, before the plague fell on his people. Recently he had been brought back... The Wampanoag's chief, Massasoit, had come with deer and other presents for the Englishmen. After a great feast and exchange of gifts, he made a treaty of peace and an alliance which were kept for fifty years by the colony, by Massasoit, and by his son, Wamsutta, whom he brought to the Englishmen..."
—Smith

As time passed hostilities increased and raids on the more isolated villages and farms took their toll. One of the most famous
"Indian" massacres occurred in Old Deerfield, Massachusetts, on
August 25, 1746. An educated slave named Lucy Terry wrote an
account—in rhyme.

August 'twas the twenty-fifth
Seventeen hundred forty-six
The Indians did in ambush lay
Some very valient men to slay
Twas nigh unto Sam Dickinson's mill,
The Indians there five men did kill
The names of whom I'll not leave out
Samuel Allen like a hero fout
And though he was so brave and bold
His face no more shall we behold
Eleazer Hawks was killed outright
Before he had time to fight
Before he did the Indians see
Was shot and killed immediately
Oliver Amsden he was slain
Which caused his friends much grief and pain
Simeon Amsden they found dead
Not many rods off from his head.
Adonijah Gillet, we do hear
Did lose his life which was so dear
John Saddler fled across the water
And so escaped the dreadful slaughter
Eunice Allen see the Indians comeing
And hoped to save herself by running
And had not her petticoats stopt her
The awful creatures had not cotched her
And tommyhawked her on the head
And left her on the ground for dead.
Young Samuel Allen, Oh! lack-a-day
Was taken and carried to Canada.
— Katz

As the natives struggled to keep their lands, they caught European diseases that wiped out whole tribes. They also found alcohol. King Hjaglar in North Carolina spoke in 1754, asking the colonists to keep the firewater away from the Native Americans.

"Brothers, here is one thing you yourselves are to blame very much in; that is you rot your grain in tubs, out of which you take and make strong spirits. You sell it to our young men and give it (to) them, many times; they get very drunk with it (and) this is the very cause that they oftentimes commit those crimes that is offensive to you and us and all through the effect of that drink. It is also very bad for our people, for it rots their guts and causes our men to get very sick and many of our people has lately died by the effects of that strong drink, and I heartily wish you would do something to prevent your people from daring to sell or give them any of that strong drink, for that...will prevent many of the abuses that is done by them through the effects of that strong drink." — *Native American Testimony*

Punishments

Visitors to colonial sites are often amused to have their photographs taken in the stocks or pillory. Being tarred and feathered might sound like a mild sort of punishment. Yet there was nothing funny about these to the colonials, especially those who had to suffer them, often for "crimes" that would not be illegal today.

For example, political or religious dissenters were ill-treated, as the following 1774 letter from a loyal British subject in Boston shows:

"...the most shocking cruelty was exercised a few Nights ago, upon a poor Man ... one Malcolm he is reckond creasy (crazy), a quarrel was pickd with him, he was afterward taken, & Tarrd, & featherd. Theres no Law that knows a punishment for the greatest Crimes beyond what this is, of cruel torture...he was stript Stark naked, one of the severest cold nights this Winter, his body coverd all over with Tar, then with feathers, his arm dislocated in tearing off his cloaths, he was draggd in a Cart with thousands attending, some beating him with clubs & Knocking him out of the Cart, then in again. They gave him several severe whipings, at different parts of the Town. This Spectacle of horror & sportive cruelty was exhibited for about five hours." — Hulton

Many of the colonists came to these shores in search of religious freedom—for themselves. They were no more tolerant of the varying beliefs of others than the Europeans had been with them in the Mother Country.

The Quakers especially came in for their share of religious persecution.

The pillory

"Let us recount the welcome of New England Christians to the first Quakers on American soil. ...Fierce laws and cruel sentences greeted them; within four years after that first appearance (1656) scores of Quakers had been stripped naked, whipped, pilloried, stocked, caged, imprisoned, branded and maimed; and four had been hanged in Boston by our Puritan forefathers...

"Here is an account of a Quaker's treatment in New Haven: 'The Drum was Beat, the People gather'd, Norton was fetch'd and stripp'd to the Waste (sic), and set with his Back to the Magistrates, and given in their View Thirty-Six cruel Stripes with a knotted cord, and his hand made fast in the Stocks where they had set his Body before, and burn'd very deep with a Red-hot Iron with H. for Heresie.' Quaker women were punished with equal ferocity.

They were banished from the colony after the punishments were carried out.

"(In early Virginia) blasphemy was punished by boring the tongue with a red hot bodkin; one offender was thus punished and chained to a tree to die." — *Curious Punishments*

"Scolding women" were placed in chairs and dunked into a pond or river several times to "cool (their) immoderate heat."

Used alone, the stocks and pillory relied more upon humiliation than physical pain. The stocks were a pair of boards with holes through which a seated person would put their feet; the pillory was a similar device with holes for the hands and sometimes the head. Passers by would tease or perhaps throw rotten vegetables at the person being punished. Sometimes, though, the punishment would include being whipped or branded as well.

"It would be impossible to enumerate the offences for which Englishmen were pilloried; among them were treason, sedition, arson, blasphemy, witch-craft, perjury, wife-beating, cheating, forging, gaming, dice-cogging, quarrelling, lying, libelling, slandering, threatening, conjuring, fortune-telling, drunkenness, impudence. One man was set in the pillory for delivering false dinner invitations; another for a rough practical joke; another for selling an injurious quack medicine. All sharpers, beggars, imposters, vagabonds, were liable to be pilloried. So fierce sometimes was the attack of the populace with various annoying and heavy missiles on pillories prisoners that several deaths are known to have ensued...

"The whipping-post was speedily in full force in Boston. At the session of the court held November 30, 1630, one man was sentenced to be whipped for stealing a loaf of bread; another for shooting fowl on the Sabbath, another for swearing, another for leaving a boat 'without a pylott...(In 1631) Philip Ratcliffe (was sentenced to) be shipped, have his eares cutt off, fined 40 pounds, and banished out of the limits of this jurisdiction for uttering malicious and scandalous speeches against the Government." — *Curious Punishments*

Nor did the children in school escape punishment. Whipping was common, often with birch rods.

"Many ingenius punishments were invented. A specially insulting one was to send the pupil out to cut a small branch of a tree. A split was made by the teacher at the severed end of the branch, and the culprit's nose was placed in the cleft end. Then he was forced to stand, painfully pinched, an object of ridicule... 'Whispering sticks' were used to preserve quiet in the school-room...wooden gags to be tied in the mouth with strings, somewhat as a bit is placed in a horse's mouth. Children were punished by being seated on a unipod, a stool with but a single leg, upon which it was most tiring to try to balance; they were made to stand on dunce stools and wear dunce caps and heavy leather spectacles; they were labeled with large placards marked with degrading or ridiculous names, such as 'Tell-Tale,' 'Bite-Finger-Baby,' ...(and) 'Idle-Boy.' " — *Child Life*

Nor were children spared even when they were playing. John Newbery's A Little Pretty Pocket-Book *was probably the first book published for children that wasn't strictly a school book. It could be bought either by itself or with a pincushion and a ball.*

The author referred to himself as "Jack the Giant Killer" and is very moralistic.

"I have here sent you A Little Pretty Pocket-Book, which will teach you to play at all those innocent games that good Boys and Girls divert themselves with: And, while you behave so well, you shall never want Play I assure you. But then, my dear Tommy, in order that you may be as good as possible, I have also sent you a Ball, the one side of which is Red, and the other Black, and with it ten Pins; and I must insist upon making this Bargain, that your Nurse may hang up the Ball by the String to it, and for every good Action you do a Pin shall be stuck on the Red Side, and for every bad Action you do a Pin shall be stuck on the Black Side. And when by doing good and pretty Things you have got all the ten Pins on the Red Side, then I'll send you a Penny, and so I will as often as all the Pins shall be fairly got on that Side. But ever the Pins be all found on the Black Side of the Ball, then I'll send a Rod, and you shall be whipt as often as they are found there. But this, my Dear, I hope you'll prevent by continuing a good Boy, that every body may still love you, as well as Your Friend, Jack the Giant-Killer.

Clearly there were few places the colonial children could escape being judged—and judged to be lacking.

Travel

Once the colonists arrived at their new homes, they were un-
likely to travel very much from one place to another over long
distances. Roads were poor or nonexistent, services along the
way primitive; it was easy to get lost, and there was often the
risk of meeting unfriendly natives.

"Travel by land in the colonies was for many years very limited in amount, and equally hazardous and inconvenient. Travel
by boat was so greatly preferred that most of the settlements continued to be made on the banks of rivers and along the seacoast.
Even perilous canoes were preferable to the miseries of land
travel..." — *Stage Coach*

As bad as transportation was, communication was even worse.
It could take months for messages to cross the ocean and days or
weeks for letters to be carried even short distances overland in the
colonies. The mail service had a faltering start and was not espe-
cially dependable.

"In unusual or violent weather the slowness of mail carriage
was appalling. Salem (Massachusetts) and Portsmouth (New
Hampshire) are about forty miles apart. In March, 1716, the
'post' took nine days for one trip between the two towns and
eight days the other. He was on snowshoes, and he reported drifts
from six to fourteen feet deep; but even so, four to five miles a
day was rather minute progress." — *Stage Coach*

An eighteenth century post rider

"The postman...was ordered to look out and report the condition of all ferries, fords and roads. He had to be 'active, stout, indefatigable, and honest.' When he delivered his mail it was laid on a table at an inn, and anyone who wished looked over all the letters, then took and paid the postage (which was very high) on any addressed to himself... As late as 1730 the mail was carried from New York to Albany in the winter by a 'footpost.' He went up the Hudson River, and lonely enough it must have been; probably he skated up when the ice was good... A Pennsylvania post-rider, an aged man, occupied himself as he slowly jogged along by knitting mittens and stockings." — *Home Life*

"The early taverns were not opened wholly for the convenience of travellers; they were for the comfort of the townspeople, for the interchange of news and opinions, the sale of solacing liquors, and the incidental sociability; in fact, the importance of the tavern to its local neighbors was far greater than to travellers. There were many restrictions upon the entertainment of unknown strangers. The landlord had to give the name of all such strangers to the selectmen, who could, if they deemed them detrimental or likely to become a charge upon the community, warn them out of the town. ..." — *Stage Coach*

"In traveling, men carried clean shirts, waistcoats, and caps, and—most interesting of all—clean sheets." — Andrews

"One landlord had the (reputation) of frequently tricking (coach) travellers who stopped for a single meal by having the driver call out 'Stage is ready' before they could eat the dinner they had ordered and paid for. A Yankee passenger disregarded this hasty summons and leisurely ate his dinner while the stage drove off without him. He finished the roast and called at last for a bowl of bread and milk to top off with as dessert. Not a spoon could be found for this dish, though plenty of silver spoons had been on the table when the stage stopped. To the distracted landlord the Yankee drawled out, 'Do you think them passengers was going away without something for their money? I could (point) out the man that took them spoons.' A stable boy on a fleet horse was promptly despatched after the stage and overtook it two miles down the road. A low-spoken explanation and request to the driver caused him to turn quickly around and drive back to the tavern door with all the angry protesting passengers. The excited landlord called out to the Yankee as the coach stopped, 'You just p'int out the man that took them spoons.' — 'Sartinly, Squire,' said he, as he climbed into the coach, 'I'll p'int him out. I took 'em myself. You'll find 'em all in the big coffee pot on the table. Hurry up, driver, I've had my dinner. All aboard.' ..." — *Stage Coach*

Bibliography

Andrews, Charles M. *Colonial Folkways, A Chronicle of American Life in the Reign of the Georges*. New Haven: Yale University Press, 1919

Annals of America, vol. 1&2. Chicago: Encyclopedia Britannica, Inc., 1968

Earle, Alice Morse. *Child Life in Colonial Days*. New York: The Macmillan Company, 1899

————*Colonial Dames and Good Wives*. New York: Frederick Ungar Publishing Co., reprinted 1962

———— *Curious Punishments of Bygone Days*. Chicago: Herbert St. Stone & Co., 1896; reprinted by Charles E. Tuttle Company, Inc., 1972

————*Home Life in Colonial Days*. (New York): The Macmillan Company, 1898. Reprinted by Corner House Publishers, 1975

————*Stage Coach and Tavern Days*. New York: The Macmillan Company, 1900

————*Two Centuries of Costume in America 1620-1820*. New York: Macmillan, 1903; Reprinted by Dover Publications, 1970

Bibliography, continued

Eggleston, George Cary. *Life in the Eighteenth Century.* New York: A.S. Barnes & Company, 1905

Fiske, John. *Dutch and Quaker Colonies in America.* Boston: Houghton, Mifflin and Company, 1899

Goodwin, Maud Wilder. *Dutch and English on the Hudson, A Chronicle of Colonial New York.* New Haven: Yale University Press, 1919

Hulton, Ann. *Letters of a Loyalist Lady 1767-1776.* Cambridge: Harvard University Press, 1927

Katz, William Loren. *Eyewitness: The Negro in American History.* New York: Pitman Publishing Corporation, 1967

Native American Testimony: A Chronicle of Indian-White Relations from Prophecy to the Present, 1492-1992, edited by Peter Nabokov. New York: Viking, 1991

Newbery, John. *A Little Pretty Pocket-Book.* London, 1767. Facsimile edition: Harcourt Brace & World, Inc., 1967

Smith, Helen Ainslie. *The Thirteen Colonies.* New York: G.P. Putnam's Sons, 1901

Suggested Further Reading

de Pauw, Linda Grant. *Founding Mothers—Women of America in the Revolutionary Era.* Boston: Houghton-Mifflin, 1975

Encyclopedia of the North American Colonies. New York: Charles Scribners' Sons, 1993

Hawke, David Freeman. *Everyday Life in Early America.* New York: Harper & Row, 1988

Washburne, Carolyn Kott. *A Multicultural Portrait of Colonial Life.* New York: Marshall Cavendish, 1994

Other Titles on Colonial History From the *Perspectives on History Series*

Faith Unfurled: The Pilgrims' Quest for Freedom

Cry "Witch": The Salem Witch Trials - 1692

Life in the Southern Colonies: Williamsburg, Jamestown, and St. Mary's City

Shot Heard 'Round the World: The Beginnings of the American Revolution

Women in the American Revolution

Principles of Democracy: The Constitution and the Bill of Rights

Colonial Triangular Trade: An Economy Based on Human Misery

About the Editor

Jeanne Munn Bracken, a reference librarian and writer, lives with her family and assorted pets on an acre in Littleton, Massachusetts, that was colonized over three centuries ago. She comes to her interest in history through the back door: by living amid the sighs and ghosts of our ancestors. History is not, she has discovered, a collection of battles and dates to memorize, but the stories of real people, whom we must recognize not for their differences from us but for their similarities to us.